Superfoods Chia S[eeds]

Quick and Easy Chia Seed Recipes for Healthy Living

Sarah Spencer

Copyrights

All rights reserved © Sarah Spencer and The Cookbook Publisher. No part of this publication or the information in it may be quoted from or reproduced in any form by means such as printing, scanning, photocopying, or otherwise without prior written permission of the copyright holder.

Disclaimer and Terms of Use

Effort has been made to ensure that the information in this book is accurate and complete. However, the author and the publisher do not warrant the accuracy of the information, text, and graphics contained within the book due to the rapidly changing nature of science, research, known and unknown facts, and internet. The author and the publisher do not hold any responsibility for errors, omissions, or contrary interpretation of the subject matter herein. This book is presented solely for motivational and informational purposes only.

The recipes provided in this book are for informational purposes only and are not intended to provide dietary advice. A medical practitioner should be consulted before making any changes in diet. Additionally, recipe cooking times may require adjustment depending on age and quality of appliances. Readers are strongly urged to take all precautions to ensure ingredients are fully cooked in order to avoid the dangers of foodborne illnesses. The recipes and suggestions provided in this book are solely the opinion of the author. The author and publisher do not take any responsibility for any consequences that may result due to following the instructions provided in this book.

ISBN: 978-1981525706

Printed in the United States

Contents

Introduction _____ 1

Breakfast Recipes _____ 5

Savory Recipes _____ 23

Salads, Sides, Snacks and Appetizers _____ 41

Dessert Recipes _____ 53

Recipe Index _____ 63

More Books by Sarah Spencer _____ 65

Appendix - Cooking Conversion Charts _____ 67

Introduction

These tiny black and white seeds have become the latest darling in the health food world for their slew of nutritional benefits. Like quinoa, chia seeds originated from parts of Mexico and South America, and were widely consumed by the Mayans and Aztec people for their 'superpower' qualities. Today, chia can still be found in the region's cuisine, including in a popular drink called chia fresca, which comprises water, chia seeds, lemon or lime juice, and a sweetener.

When eaten dry, chia has a mild, nutty flavor and crunchy texture that gives it a similar taste profile to a poppy seed. However, this changes after the seeds are hydrated, because they act as a sponge and absorb liquid up to 10 times their weight to form gel-like globules that have a thickening effect. Such unique qualities make chia seed a versatile ingredient to be used in recipes, rather than purely taken as a supplement.

One of the most popular ways to enjoy chia is to make a chia pudding by simply soaking the seeds with water, milk, or juice for at least 15 minutes. Jazz it up with your favorite spices, chopped fruits, nuts, or any desired toppings. Chia can be used to thicken food by adding bulk and nutrition to a dish without piling on empty calories. Its mild taste means that its addition is unlikely to affect the overall taste of the dish.

For baking, substitute eggs in the recipe with chia gel to make it vegan. Mix one part chia seed to six parts water to create the chia gel; one tablespoon of this chia gel is equivalent to one large egg. Interestingly, you can also grow chia sprouts at home (using the seeds) for some homegrown sprouts to enjoy with your salad. This book explores many more creative ways to incorporate chia seeds in your food routine, from mixing them into curries, to using them as a breadcrumb substitute.

These super seeds are well worth your time and money if you are making an effort to eat healthier. For starters, they are an unprocessed, whole grain food, a high fiber option that will leave you fuller for a longer period of time while reducing the risk of constipation. Furthermore, they are also a nutrition powerhouse compared to other foods – a good source of not only omega-3 fatty acids that keep the heart and brain healthy, but also protein which is necessary for cell regeneration. Studies have shown that the antioxidant activity is higher in chia seed than any other whole food, including blueberries. Antioxidants are required for the prevention of cellular damage that often leads to aging, cancer, and other illnesses.

Given the host of health benefits, it is time to incorporate chia seed as an ingredient into your home cooking to eat well and feel better. Start flipping through the recipes inside this book to get inspiration for your next dish today!

Tips for buying and storing

Chia seeds sold in stores are always vegetarian and gluten free, which is great for those on plant-based diets, and people who have celiac disease. However, not all brands are organic or GMO-free. Check the packaging to make sure they are certified.

When selecting chia seeds, appearance is key. The tiny seeds should be either speckled black or white; these are nutritionally similar with no differences apart from the aesthetic. However, avoid purchasing chia seeds that are yellow or brown in color, which is a sign that the seeds had failed to mature properly. Taste-wise, brown chia seeds are bitter compared to their counterparts, which tend to be slightly nutty. Furthermore, their nutrition content is also compromised, with lower levels of omega-3 and other nutrients. It is therefore crucial when purchasing chia seeds, to go for those packages that contain mostly grayish black or white seeds.

Store the chia seeds in a jar with a tight-fitting lid. Place them in a cool and dry place in the pantry, or keep them in the refrigerator for years. The same storage method can also be used for ground chia, which you can simply make by blending up your chia seeds. If you intend to make chia gel, add one part seeds to six parts water and give it a good stir. (Avoid adding water to seeds, which will result in the seeds clumping to the bottom of the jar.) Transfer the chia gel to a tightly lidded jar and store it in the refrigerator for up to 2 weeks.

Breakfast Recipes

Apple Chia Oatmeal

Servings: 4

Ingredients
¼ cup chia seeds
4 cups almond milk
2 teaspoons cinnamon
½ cup oats
3 apples, cored and diced
4 tablespoons maple syrup

Preparation
1. In a medium saucepan, combine the chia seeds, almond milk, cinnamon, and oats. Bring the mixture to a boil over medium heat and cook until the chia seeds and oats thicken to the desired consistency, about 2-3 minutes.
2. Divide the oatmeal into four portions. Finish with the diced apples and a generous drizzle of maple syrup.

Nutritional Facts (317 g per single serving)
Calories 287
Fats 10 g
Carbs 45 g
Protein 6 g
Sodium 101 mg

Overnight Chia and Berry Parfait

Servings: 1

Ingredients
½ cup Greek yogurt
2 tablespoons chia seeds
2 tablespoons oats
3 tablespoons milk
4 tablespoons frozen mixed berries
1 tablespoon almond butter
1 teaspoon honey

Preparation
1. In an 8 ounce canning jar or medium-sized bowl, combine the yogurt, chia seeds, oats, milk, and berries.
2. Top the mixture with almond butter and honey.
3. Leave the chia and oat parfait in the refrigerator overnight, before enjoying it the next day.

Nutritional Facts (296 g per single serving)
Calories 552
Fats 29 g
Carbs 25 g
Protein 53 g
Sodium 69 mg

Tropical Chia Seed Breakfast Bowl

Servings: 1

Ingredients
3 tablespoons chia seeds
⅔ cup almond milk
Pinch salt
1 tablespoon maple syrup
1 tablespoon toasted shredded coconut
1 tablespoon pumpkin seeds
1 passion fruit, halved

Preparation
1. In a medium bowl, stir together the chia seeds and almond milk. Set it aside for 15 minutes to allow the chia seeds to thicken.
2. Stir in the salt and maple syrup.
3. Serve with shredded coconut, pumpkin seeds, and the juice and seeds of the passion fruit.

Nutritional Facts (233 g per single serving)
Calories 200
Fats 23 g
Carbs 5 g
Protein 5 g
Sodium 289 mg

Gluten-Free Blueberry Chia Pancakes

Servings: 5

Ingredients
1 cup oat flour
3 teaspoons baking powder
¼ teaspoon salt
1 ⅓ cups almond milk
1 egg
2 teaspoons vanilla extract
2 tablespoons chia seeds
½ cup fresh blueberries
Oil, for greasing
Optional toppings: butter, maple syrup, fresh blueberries

Preparation
1. In a large bowl, whisk together the oat flour, baking powder, and salt.
2. In another bowl, mix the almond milk, egg, and vanilla extract.
3. Combine the wet ingredients with the dry ingredients until they are just combined and still lumpy.
4. Fold the chia seeds and blueberries into the batter.
5. Grease a griddle or medium skillet with oil, and heat over medium-low.
6. Spoon a ¼ cup of batter into the skillet and allow it to cook until bubbles start to form in the pancake and the bottom turns golden brown. Flip it over and cook for another minute or two.
7. Serve immediately with butter, maple syrup, and other desired toppings.

Nutritional Facts (50 g per single serving)
Calories 110
Fats 3 g
Carbs 17 g
Protein 4 g
Sodium 167 mg

Basic Almond Chia Granola

Makes: 5 cups

Ingredients
2 cups rolled oats
¾ cup raw almonds, roughly chopped
½ cup chia seeds
½ cup shredded unsweetened coconut
½ teaspoon salt
⅓ cup honey
⅓ cup coconut oil
1 tablespoon brown sugar
1 teaspoon vanilla extract
1 egg white

Preparation
1. Preheat the oven to 300ºF. Line a 9x13 baking sheet with parchment paper.
2. In a large bowl, combine the oats, almonds, chia seeds, shredded coconut, and salt.
3. In a small bowl, whisk together the honey, coconut oil, brown sugar, vanilla extract, and egg white.
4. Add the wet ingredients to the dry ingredients and stir to coat everything well.
5. Transfer the mixture to the prepared baking sheet and spread it around.
6. Bake for about 45 minutes, stirring twice throughout the baking process.
7. Allow the granola to cool before storing it in an airtight container.

Nutritional Facts (167 g per single cup serving)
Calories 925
Fats 69 g
Carbs 67 g
Protein 21 g
Sodium 295 mg

Chia and Egg Breakfast Cups

Servings: 6

Ingredients
4 large eggs
4 egg whites
1 large Roma tomato, diced
10 ounces fresh spinach, cooked
1 medium onion, diced
2 tablespoons fresh parsley, finely chopped
2 tablespoons chia seeds
¼ teaspoon sea salt
¼ teaspoon pepper
Non-stick cooking spray

Preparation
1. Preheat the oven to 350ºF. Grease a 6-hole muffin tin with non-stick cooking spray.
2. In large bowl, whisk together the eggs, egg whites, tomatoes, spinach, onion, parsley, chia seeds, salt, and pepper.
3. Transfer the egg mixture to the prepared muffin tins.
4. Bake for 30 minutes, or until the egg is cooked through.
5. Set the breakfast cups aside to cool for at least 10 minutes before digging in.

Nutritional Facts (148 g per single serving)
Calories 110
Fats 5 g
Carbs 7 g
Protein 9 g
Sodium 197 mg

Banana Walnut Chia Bread

Servings: 8

Ingredients

1 tablespoon chia seeds
3 tablespoons water
2 ripe bananas, peeled and mashed
¼ cup low-fat milk
2 tablespoons maple syrup
½ cup unsweetened shredded coconut
1 cup all-purpose flour
¼ cup superfine sugar
1 teaspoon baking powder
¼ cup walnut, roughly crushed
Non-stick cooking spray

Preparation

1. Preheat the oven to 350°F. Line a loaf pan with parchment paper and grease it with non-stick cooking spray.
2. In a small cup, stir the chia seeds and water together. Set them aside for 15-20 minutes to thicken.
3. Meanwhile, mix the bananas, milk, and maple syrup in a small bowl.
4. In a large bowl, whisk together the shredded coconut, flour, sugar, and baking powder.
5. Add the banana mixture to the dry ingredients. Pour in the chia seeds and mix until just combined. Fold in the walnuts.
6. Transfer the batter to the prepared pan. Bake for 45 minutes, or until a skewer comes out clean when inserted into the thickest part of the bread.

7. Remove the bread from the oven, and allow it to sit in the pan for 10 minutes. Take the bread out of the pan and let it cool completely on a wire rack.

Nutritional Facts (76 g per single serving)
Calories 251
Fats 13 g
Carbs 33 g
Protein 4 g
Sodium 11 mg

Whole Wheat Chia Waffles

Servings: 8

Ingredients
2 cups almond milk
1 teaspoon vinegar
1 cup whole wheat flour
¾ cup spelt flour
1 tablespoon baking powder
½ teaspoon baking soda
¼ teaspoon salt
2 tablespoons chia seeds
2 tablespoons flax meal
Non-stick cooking spray

Preparation
1. In a medium bowl, stir together the almond milk and vinegar. Set it aside for 5 minutes to make buttermilk.
2. In a large bowl, whisk together the whole wheat flour, spelt flour, baking powder, baking soda, and salt.
3. Add the chia seeds and flax meal to the almond milk.
4. Incorporate the wet ingredients into the dry ingredients, and mix until just combined.
5. Heat the waffle iron and lightly grease it with non-stick cooking spray. Scoop a ladle of the batter onto the waffle iron and cook the waffle as per the manufacturer's instructions.

Nutritional Facts (103 g per single serving)
Calories 147
Fats 4 g
Carbs 25 g
Protein 6 g
Sodium 122 mg

Eggless French Toast

Servings: 2

Ingredients
1 tablespoon chia seeds
½ tablespoon maple syrup
1 cup unsweetened almond milk
½ teaspoon ground cinnamon
½ teaspoon vanilla extract
1 tablespoon coconut oil
4 slices bread
Optional toppings: Whipped cream, maple syrup, fresh fruits

Preparation
1. In a small bowl, stir together the chia seeds, maple syrup, almond milk, cinnamon, and vanilla extract. Set the mixture aside for 20 minutes for the chia seeds to thicken.
2. Heat the coconut oil in a griddle or skillet over medium heat.
3. Pour the chia seed mixture into a large casserole dish. Dip the bread slices into the mixture, remembering to coat it on both sides.
4. Transfer the toast to the griddle or skillet, and cook for 3-4 minutes on each side, or until it turns golden brown.
5. Serve immediately with your favorite toppings.

Nutritional Facts (210 g per single serving)
Calories 295
Fats 14 g
Carbs 36 g
Protein 9 g
Sodium 372 mg

Peanut Butter and Chocolate Chia Muffins

Servings: 12

Ingredients

1 cup rolled oats
1 cup all-purpose flour
½ teaspoon salt
1 tablespoon baking powder
½ cup honey
½ cup creamy peanut butter, room temperature
1 cup unsweetened almond milk
2 eggs
¼ cup melted coconut oil
1 tablespoon chia seeds
⅓ cup chocolate chips

Preparation

1. Preheat the oven to 400°F. Line a 12-cup muffin tin with cupcake liners.
2. In a large bowl, whisk together the oats, flour, salt, and baking powder.
3. In a medium bowl, mix the honey, peanut butter, almond milk, eggs, and coconut oil, until they are well incorporated.
4. Add the dry ingredients into the wet ingredients and mix until just combined.
5. Stir in the chia seeds and chocolate chips. Portion the batter into the prepared muffin cups.
6. Bake for 15 minutes, or until a toothpick comes out clean when inserted into the thickest part of the muffin.
7. Remove the pan from the oven and allow the muffins to rest in the tin for 10 minutes. Transfer the muffins to a wire rack to cool completely.

Nutritional Facts *(96 g per single serving)*
Calories 320
Fats 17 g
Carbs 34 g
Protein 10 g
Sodium 238 mg

Chia Seed Omelette with Mushrooms and Asparagus

Servings: 1

Ingredients
1 tablespoon chia seeds
2 tablespoons water
2 eggs
4 asparagus spears
4 brown mushrooms, sliced
1 tablespoon butter
Salt and pepper, to taste

Preparation
1. In a small bowl, stir together the chia seeds and water. Set them aside for 20 minutes for the chia seeds to thicken up.
2. In a medium bowl, whisk together the eggs and chia mixture. Season with salt and pepper.
3. Place the asparagus spears in a steamer and cook for about a minute. Alternatively, place them in the microwave, covered with plastic wrap, and heat on high for 30 seconds.
4. Heat half the butter in a skillet over medium heat. Add the mushrooms and cook them for 5 minutes. Season with salt and pepper, and transfer them to a clean plate.
5. Heat the rest of the butter. Pour the egg mixture into the skillet and cook until it is about to set, about 3-5 minutes. Place the asparagus and mushrooms in the center of the egg.
6. Fold the egg in half and serve immediately.

Nutritional Facts (276 g per single serving)
Calories 363
Fats 28 g
Carbs 13 g
Protein 18 g
Sodium 153 mg

Creamy Blueberry, Chia, and Coconut Smoothie

Servings: 2

Ingredients
1 ½ cups coconut milk
½ cup soft tofu
1 tablespoon honey
2 tablespoons chia seeds
1 tablespoon vanilla whey protein powder
1 cup frozen blueberries

Preparation
1. Throw all the ingredients into a blender and whizz it up until the mixture becomes smooth and creamy. Serve immediately.

Nutritional Facts (192 g per single serving)
Calories 248
Fats 13 g
Carbs 27 g
Protein 11 g
Sodium 18 mg

Peach and Chia Seeds Smoothie

Servings: 2

Ingredients
¼ cup oats
2 ripe peaches, stones removed
1 tablespoon chia seeds
½ frozen medium banana
¼ cup fresh orange juice
½ cup unsweetened almond milk

Preparation
1. In a blender, blitz the oats up for a minute or two to break them down into smaller pieces.
2. Add the rest of the ingredients to the blender and combine until the mixture reaches a smooth consistency.

Nutritional Facts (271 g per single serving)
Calories 260
Fats 10 g
Carbs 41 g
Protein 8 g
Sodium 84 mg

Raspberry Chia Seed Jam

Makes: 1 ½ cups

Ingredients
1 cup raspberries
1 tablespoon chia seeds
2 tablespoons water
2 tablespoons honey

Preparation
1. Mix the chia seeds with the water in a small cup. Set it aside for 10 minutes so the chia seeds can thicken.
2. In a blender, mix the raspberries, chia mixture, and honey together.
3. Transfer the jam to a jar and store it in the refrigerator for up to a week.

Nutritional Facts per jar (213 g serving)
Calories 278
Fats 7 g
Carbs 57 g
Protein 4 g
Sodium 6 mg

Spiced Plum and Pear Chia Seed Jam

Servings: 2 pints

Ingredients
1 pound ripe pears, peeled, cored and diced
1 pound ripe plums, peeled, pitted and diced
1 tablespoon fresh ginger, minced
⅓ cup maple syrup
¼ cup chia seeds

Preparation
1. In a medium saucepan, bring the pears, plums, ginger, and maple syrup to a boil over medium-high heat. Once it reaches a boil, reduce the heat to medium and cook until the fruit becomes soft and mushy, about 25-30 minutes.
2. Using the back of a fork, mash the mixture up. Stir in the chia seeds and remove it from heat. Set it aside to let it cool completely.
3. Store it in a clean jar, refrigerated, for up to 2 weeks.

Nutritional Facts per jar (619 g serving)
Calories 450
Fats 10 g
Carbs 93 g
Protein 8 g
Sodium 9 mg

Savory Recipes

Chia Crusted Baked Tilapia

Servings: 4

Ingredients
¾ cup cornmeal
½ teaspoon chia seeds
½ teaspoon garlic powder
Salt and pepper, to taste
1 ½ tablespoons low fat mayonnaise
4 boneless tilapia fillets, patted dry
Non-stick cooking spray

Preparation
1. Preheat the oven to 400ºF. Line a baking sheet with parchment paper and grease it with non-stick cooking spray.
2. In a small bowl, mix together the cornmeal, chia seeds, and garlic powder; season with salt and pepper to taste.
3. Spread a thin layer of mayonnaise on both sides of each fillet. Coat them with the cornmeal mixture, making sure to press in the mixture to help it stick.
4. Transfer the fillets to the baking sheet. Bake for 15-20 minutes.

Nutritional Facts (146 g per single serving)
Calories 221
Fats 6 g
Carbs 18 g
Protein 25 g
Sodium 114 mg

Salmon and Haddock Chia Fish Cakes

Servings: 4

Ingredients
2 large salmon fillets, skinless and roughly chopped
1 haddock fillet
2 teaspoons Dijon mustard, divided
3 tablespoons fresh chives, chopped
1 tablespoon chia seeds
1 spring onion, finely chopped
1 tablespoon capers
1 lemon, zest and juice, divided
Salt and pepper
½ green cabbage
⅓ cup plain yogurt
1 tablespoon coconut oil

Preparation
1. In a food processor, blend together the salmon, haddock, 1 teaspoon of Dijon mustard, chives, chia seeds, spring onion, capers, and lemon zest. Season with salt and pepper.
2. Divide the mixture into four equal portions and shape them into patties. Place them in the freezer for 5 minutes to firm up.
3. Meanwhile, make the coleslaw. Slice the cabbage into long strips and place it in a medium bowl. Toss it with the remaining teaspoon of Dijon mustard, lemon juice, and yogurt
4. Heat the coconut oil in a large skillet over medium-high heat. Fry the fish patties on both sides, about 6 minutes in total.
5. Serve immediately with the slaw on the side.

Nutritional Facts (387 g per single serving)
Calories 411
Fats 18 g
Carbs 10 g
Protein 50 g
Sodium 269 mg

Chicken Chia Nuggets

Servings: 4

Ingredients
1 pound boneless skinless chicken breast, cut into nugget-sized pieces
¾ cup ground flax seed
¼ cup chia seeds
¼ cup Parmesan cheese, grated
1 teaspoon salt
1 teaspoon oregano
½ teaspoon basil
2 cloves garlic, minced
2 eggs, lightly beaten
Non-stick cooking spray

Preparation
1. Preheat the oven to 400°F. Lightly grease a baking sheet with non-stick cooking spray.
2. In a medium bowl, whisk together the flax seed, chia seeds, Parmesan, salt, oregano, basil, and garlic.
3. Dip each nugget into the egg, and then coat it in the chia and flax seed mixture. Arrange the pieces on the prepared baking sheet. Repeat until all the chicken is covered with the mixture.
4. Bake for 25 minutes, or until the chicken is lightly brown and cooked through. While baking, turn the chicken pieces over once to cook evenly on both sides.

Nutritional Facts (180 g per single serving)
Calories 366
Fats 19 g
Carbs 13 g
Protein 36 g
Sodium 788 mg

Chia Breaded Chicken Breast

Servings: 4

Ingredients
¾ cup Italian seasoned breadcrumbs
½ cup chia seeds
¼ cup shredded Parmesan cheese
1 tablespoon dried parsley flakes
½ teaspoon salt
4 boneless, skinless chicken breasts
Non-stick cooking spray

Preparation
1. Preheat the oven to 375°F. Lightly grease a baking sheet with non-stick cooking spray.
2. In a medium bowl, whisk together the breadcrumbs, chia seeds, Parmesan, parsley flakes, and salt.
3. Coat the chicken breasts with the breadcrumbs and press it in gently so the coating sticks to the meat. Bake for 25 minutes, or until the chicken is completely cooked through.
4. Allow the chicken to rest for 5 minutes before cutting it into slices.

Nutritional Facts (331 g per single serving)
Calories 583
Fats 19 g
Carbs 29 g
Protein 71 g
Sodium 831 mg

Red Curry Chicken with Chia

Servings: 4

Ingredients
1 pound skinless, boneless chicken thighs, cut into bite-size pieces
1 (15 ounce) can full fat coconut milk
2 cups water
1 cup basmati rice
1 tablespoon vegetable oil
½ red chili, thinly chopped
3 cloves garlic, thinly chopped
2 tablespoons red curry paste
1 red bell pepper, thinly sliced
½ head broccoli, cut into small pieces
6 scallions, thinly chopped
½ cup chicken stock
3 tablespoons soy sauce
1 tablespoon fish sauce
1 tablespoon palm sugar
Zest and juice of 1 lime
2 tablespoons chia seeds

Preparation
1. In a large bowl, toss the chicken pieces with the coconut milk. Set it aside to marinate for at least 10 minutes.
2. Bring the water to a boil in a large saucepan. Add the rice, and cook for about 12-15 minutes, or until most of the water is absorbed. Remove it from the heat, cover the pot with a lid, and allow the rice to steam for 5 minutes.
3. In a wok or a large skillet, heat the vegetable oil over medium-high heat. Cook the garlic and chili for 30 seconds before adding the curry paste. Fry the paste for about a minute, until it becomes fragrant and the chili oil is released.
4. Pour about ½ cup of the coconut milk from the bowl with the chicken into the wok to thin the paste out. Mix well.

5. Add the bell pepper, broccoli, and chicken, reserving the rest of the coconut milk. Cook for about 4 minutes.
6. Throw in the scallions to fry for 1 minute.
7. Pour in the rest of the coconut milk, chicken stock, soy sauce, fish sauce, palm sugar, and the lime zest and juice. Bring the mixture to a low simmer, stirring frequently to prevent the coconut milk from curdling.
8. Remove the skillet from the heat and stir in the chia seeds.
9. Fluff the rice, and serve it with the curry.

Nutritional Facts (339 g per single serving)
Calories 665
Fats 37 g
Carbs 55 g
Protein 33 g
Sodium 716 mg

Beef and Broccoli Stir Fry

Servings: 4

Ingredients
1 pound sirloin beef strips
1 ½ tablespoons cornstarch
¼ teaspoon salt
¼ teaspoon black pepper
½ teaspoon ground ginger
3 tablespoons vegetable oil, divided
10 ounces frozen broccoli florets
1 small onion, sliced
3 cloves garlic, chopped
3 tablespoons soy sauce
⅓ cup water
1 tablespoon chia seeds
1 tablespoon flax seeds
1 tablespoon sesame seeds

Preparation
1. In a large bowl, toss the beef strips with the cornstarch, salt, pepper, and ground ginger.
2. In a large skillet or wok, heat 2 tablespoons of oil over medium-high heat. Add the beef and cook for 2 minutes. Transfer the beef to a clean plate and keep it warm.
3. Heat the remaining oil. Cook the broccoli, onion, and garlic for about 2 minutes, or until the broccoli is slightly tender.
4. Mix in the soy sauce and water. Cover the skillet and allow the liquid to bubble. Return the beef to the sauce, and sprinkle in the three types of seeds. Stir, and cook until the sauce becomes thicker, about 2 minutes.
5. Serve immediately.

Nutritional Facts (269 g per single serving)
Calories 416
Fats 32 g
Carbs 13 g
Protein 26 g
Sodium 884 mg

Meatloaf with Chia Seeds

Servings: 4

Ingredients
1 pound ground beef
1 egg
½ cup ketchup, divided
1 teaspoon Worcestershire sauce
2 tablespoons finely chopped onion
1 ½ tablespoons chia seeds
⅓ cup chicken stock
½ cup frozen spinach, thawed and squeezed dry
½ cup shredded carrots
Salt and pepper, to taste
1 tablespoon honey

Preparation
1. Preheat the oven to 350°F.
2. In a large bowl, combine the ground beef, egg, ¼ cup ketchup, Worcestershire sauce, onion, chia seeds, chicken stock, spinach, carrots, salt, and pepper until well combined. Transfer the mixture into a loaf pan.
3. In a small bowl, stir the remaining ketchup together with the honey.
4. Bake for 30 minutes and remove it from the oven. Drain any accumulated grease, and spread the ketchup and honey all over the top of the meatloaf.
5. Return the pan to the oven and bake for another 15-20 minutes, or until the meat is cooked through.

Nutritional Facts (227 g per single serving)
Calories 357
Fats 32 g
Carbs 11 g
Protein 24 g
Sodium 395 mg

Pulled Pork with Barbecue Chia Seed Sauce

Servings: 6

Ingredients
1 (15 ounce) can tomato sauce
2 tablespoons tomato paste
½ cup apple cider vinegar
2 tablespoons honey
2 tablespoons Worcestershire sauce
1 teaspoon sweet paprika
1 teaspoon ground mustard
½ teaspoon chipotle powder
2 teaspoons sea salt
1 teaspoon pepper
½ cup chia seeds
3 pounds boneless pork shoulder
1 large onion, chopped
4 cloves garlic, minced

Preparation
1. In a large bowl, whisk together the tomato sauce, tomato paste, vinegar, honey, Worcestershire sauce, paprika, mustard, chipotle powder, salt, pepper and chia seeds.
2. Place the pork shoulder in a 5-quart slow cooker. Pour the liquid mixture all over the meat and top it off with the onions and garlic. Cover with lid and cook on high for 6 hours or on low for 10 hours.
3. Remove the pork from the slow cooker and place it inside a casserole dish or on a large serving plate. Shred the meat up with two forks.
4. Scoop the sauce all over the pulled pork to keep it moist and juicy. Best served warm.

Nutritional Facts (380 g per single serving)
Calories 446
Fats 14 g
Carbs 23 g
Protein 56 g
Sodium 1310 mg

Berry and Spinach Salad with Chia Seed Vinaigrette

Servings: 6

Ingredients
6 cups baby spinach
3 avocadoes, pitted, halved, and diced
1 cup sliced strawberries
1 cup blueberries
½ cup sliced almonds

Dressing:
½ cup olive oil
¼ cup cider vinegar
1 teaspoon Dijon mustard
½ teaspoon dried thyme
1 tablespoon chia seeds
Salt and pepper, to taste

Preparation
1. In a small bowl, whisk together all the dressing ingredients.
2. Combine the spinach, avocado, strawberries, and blueberries in a large bowl.
3. Pour the dressing all over the salad and toss to combine.
4. Serve immediately, with sliced almonds on top.

Nutritional Facts (229 g per single serving)
Calories 455
Fats 42 g
Carbs 20 g
Protein 7 g
Sodium 33 mg

Lamb Shank with Chia Seeds

Servings: 4

Ingredients
4 ½ pounds lamb shanks
2 tablespoons olive oil
3 cups shallots, peeled, whole
3 cloves garlic, roughly chopped
1 ½ teaspoons ground ginger
2 teaspoons ground cumin
½ teaspoon ground cinnamon
½ teaspoon ground cloves
4 cups chicken stock
1 (15 ounce) can chopped tomatoes
2 tablespoons tomato paste
3 tablespoons chia seeds
½ pound carrots, peeled and chopped into bite-sized pieces
1 large cinnamon stick
Pinch of sea salt

Preparation
1. Preheat the oven to 320°F.
2. Trim off all excess fat from the lamb shanks.
3. In a large skillet, heat the olive oil over medium heat. Cook the whole shallots and garlic for about 2-3 minutes. Add the spices and fry until fragrant, about 2 minutes.
4. Brown the lamb shanks on all sides, about 3-4 minutes on each side. Transfer the meat, together with all the ingredients in the skillet, into an oven-safe Dutch oven.
5. Add the rest of the ingredients to the Dutch oven. Cut a piece of parchment paper and place it on top of the meat. Cover the Dutch oven with a lid.

6. Bake for 4 ½ hours, or until the meat is tender and falls off the bone.
7. Best served warm.

Nutritional Facts (537 g per single serving)
Calories 420
Fats 13 g
Carbs 22 g
Protein 55 g
Sodium 460 mg

Mushroom Pizza with Chia Seed Crust

Servings: 4

Ingredients
2 ½ cups white whole wheat flour
¼ cup chia seeds
3 teaspoons baking powder
3 teaspoons dried basil
½ teaspoon garlic powder
1 tablespoon olive oil
1 ½ cups warm water
½ (15 ounce) can whole or diced tomatoes, drain the liquid
6 cloves garlic
2 teaspoons balsamic vinegar
Salt and pepper, to taste
Olive oil
¼ pound sliced mushrooms (brown, white, porcini or any desired mushrooms)
6 ounces mozzarella
3 tablespoons Parmesan cheese

Preparation
1. Preheat the oven to 400ºF.
2. In a medium bowl, whisk together the flour, chia seeds, baking powder, basil, and garlic powder.
3. Add the oil and water to the dry ingredients and mix them until it comes together to form a dough.
4. Tip the dough out on a clean surface and knead until it becomes slightly elastic, about 2-4 minutes. Roll the dough out in a circle.
5. Lightly grease a pizza pan with olive oil. Transfer the dough to the dish and bake for 10-12 minutes.

6. Meanwhile, make the pizza sauce. In a food processor, pulse together the tomatoes, garlic, vinegar, salt, pepper, and a drizzle of olive oil until it becomes smooth. Taste to make sure it is to your liking, and adjust if necessary.
7. Spread the pizza sauce on the pizza crust. Scatter the mushrooms and two cheeses over the top. Bake for another 8-10 minutes, or until the cheese has melted and turned golden brown.

Nutritional Facts (365 g per single serving)
Calories 530
Fats 21 g
Carbs 68 g
Protein 25 g
Sodium 466 mg

Lentils and Chia Seed Stew

Servings: 4

Ingredients
2 tablespoons olive oil
1 large white onion, diced
1 teaspoon cumin seeds
¼ teaspoon ground cardamom
1 teaspoon garlic, minced
2 teaspoons ginger, minced
2 teaspoons ground turmeric
½ fresh jalapeño, seeds removed, finely diced
4 cups water
3 ½ cups vegetable stock
2 cups red lentils
1 (15 ounce) can crushed tomatoes
1 teaspoon kosher salt
1 tablespoon chia seeds
4 tablespoons chopped cilantro
Cooked brown rice for serving

Preparation
1. In a large skillet, heat the oil over medium heat. Sauté the onion until it is lightly browned, about 10 minutes. Add the cumin seeds, cardamom, and garlic, and fry until fragrant, about 2 minutes.
2. Add the ginger, turmeric, jalapeño, water, vegetable stock, lentils, and tomatoes. Bring the pot to a boil and lower the heat to low. Simmer, covered, for 15 minutes, or until the lentils become tender.
3. Remove the pot from the heat. Stir in the salt, chia seeds, and cilantro.
4. Serve immediately with brown rice.

Nutritional Facts (686 g per single serving)
Calories 484
Fats 11 g
Carbs 76 g
Protein 27 g
Sodium 2523 mg

Baked Beef and Chia Meatballs

Servings: 6

Ingredients
1 pound 90% lean ground beef
1 large egg, beaten
1 medium carrot, grated
2 tablespoons chia seeds
½ cup fresh basil leaves, roughly chopped
¼ cup grated Parmesan cheese
2 green onions, white and light green parts, finely chopped
1 clove garlic, minced
½ teaspoon kosher salt
¼ teaspoon pepper
1 (24 ounce) jar pasta sauce

Preparation
1. Preheat the oven to 400°F.
2. In a large bowl, mix together the beef, egg, carrot, chia seeds, basil leaves, cheese, onions, garlic, salt, and pepper. Portion the meat mixture into 24 parts and roll them into balls. Arrange them in an oven-safe casserole dish and bake for 10 minutes.
3. Pour the pasta sauce into the casserole dish. Continue baking for another 20 minutes, until the sauce becomes hot and bubbly and the meatballs are cooked through.

Nutritional Facts (222 g per single serving)
Calories 296
Fats 13 g
Carbs 6 g
Protein 75 g
Sodium 835 mg

Superfood Burger Patties

Servings: 6

Ingredients
6 teaspoons extra virgin olive oil, divided
1 large onion, chopped
1 tablespoon minced garlic
10 ounces cremini mushrooms, sliced
1 cup cooked puy lentils
2 cups cooked quinoa
⅓ cup chia seeds
2 eggs
1 ½ cups grated carrot
½ cup + 2 tablespoons panko crumbs
Serve with: Burger buns, lettuce, tomato slices

Preparation
1. In a small skillet, heat 2 teaspoons of oil over medium heat. Cook the onion, garlic, and mushrooms until most of the liquid from the mushrooms has evaporated, about 5 minutes. Transfer the mixture to a food processor.
2. Add the lentils to the food processor. Pulse the ingredients until most of the ingredients a coarse mixture. Transfer to a large mixing bowl.
3. Cover a large baking sheet with plastic wrap and sprinkle 2 tablespoons of panko all over it.
4. Incorporate the quinoa, chia seeds, eggs, carrot, and ½ cup of panko to the mushroom and lentil mixture. Mix until everything comes together.
5. Divide the mixture into 6 portions, and shape them into patties. Cover the patties with another piece of plastic wrap, and put them in the refrigerator for 20 minutes to firm up.

6. Heat 4 teaspoons of oil over medium heat in a large skillet. Cook the patties for about 5 minutes on each side, or until they are golden brown.
7. Serve with burger buns, lettuce, tomato, and any of your favorite garnishes.

Nutritional Facts (214 g per single serving)
Calories 388
Fats 22 g
Carbs 39 g
Protein 12 g
Sodium 215 mg

Salads, Sides, Snacks and Appetizers

Cauliflower Chia Soup

Servings: 2

Ingredients
1 tablespoon vegetable oil
1 small onion, diced
½ head large cauliflower, chopped into small pieces
2 cups vegetable stock
Salt and pepper, to taste
1 tablespoon freshly ground chia seeds

Preparation
1. In a large saucepan, heat the oil over medium heat. Sauté the onions until they become translucent, about 3-4 minutes.
2. Add the cauliflower and vegetable stock. Bring the mixture to a boil and reduce the heat to low. Simmer, covered, for another 15 minutes, or until the cauliflower is tender.
3. Stir in the ground chia seeds. Using an immersion blender, purée the cauliflower until it becomes creamy. Season with salt and pepper.

Nutritional Facts (482 g per single serving)
Calories 179
Fats 11 g
Carbs 20 g
Protein 7 g
Sodium 720 mg

Sugar Snap Peas and Green Bean Chia Salad

Servings: 1

Ingredients
⅓ cup sugar snap peas
⅓ cup green beans
⅛ cup arugula
1 tablespoon chia seeds
Zest and juice of 1 lemon
2 tablespoons olive oil
Pinch of sea salt

Preparation
1. Steam the peas and green beans for 4-5 minutes, until crisp tender.
2. Transfer them to a medium bowl, and combine them with the arugula and chia seeds.
3. Toss the greens with lemon zest, lemon juice, olive oil, and salt to taste. Serve immediately.

Nutritional Facts (197 g per single serving)
Calories 559
Fats 35 g
Carbs 54 g
Protein 16 g
Sodium 19 mg

Grilled Fruits and Vegetable with Zesty Chia Dressing

Servings: 4

Ingredients
3 large nectarines, halved and pitted
1 large red onion, sliced into rings
1 eggplant, cut into ½-inch slices
Olive oil and salt
2 cups cooked quinoa
1 cup cooked black beans, drained and rinsed
1 cup chopped flat-leaf parsley
½ cup sliced fresh basil leaves

Dressing:
½ cup fresh orange juice
3 tablespoons fresh lime juice
2 tablespoons olive oil
1 tablespoon chia seeds
1 clove garlic, minced
½ teaspoon ground cumin
½ teaspoon salt

Preparation
1. In a small bowl, whisk together all the dressing ingredients. Set it aside to thicken for at least 15 minutes.
2. Preheat a grill pan over medium-high heat. Brush the nectarines, onion rings, and eggplant with olive oil and season with salt. Cook the nectarines for about 2 minutes. Brown the onions and eggplants for 3 minutes on each side. Let the vegetables cool down before slicing them into bite-sized pieces.

3. In a large bowl, combine the quinoa, black beans, parsley, and basil leaves with the grilled vegetables.
4. Pour the dressing over the salad and toss to combine. Serve immediately.

Nutritional Facts (485 g per single serving)
Calories 367
Fats 11 g
Carbs 60 g
Protein 12 g
Sodium 303 mg

Blackberry Oat Bars

Servings: 12

Ingredients
12 ounces blackberries
¼ cup chia seeds
1 ½ tablespoons granulated sugar
1 cup rolled oats
1 ½ cups whole wheat flour
¼ cup unsweetened shredded coconut
½ teaspoon salt
½ teaspoon baking soda
½ cup coconut oil, melted
¼ cup maple syrup
¼ cup honey

Preparation
1. Using the back of a fork, mash the blackberries into small chunks. Stir in the chia seeds and granulated sugar. Set this aside to allow the compote to thicken for 30 minutes.
2. Preheat the oven to 350°F. Line an 8x8 pan with parchment paper, and grease it with coconut oil.
3. In a large bowl, whisk together the oats, flour, shredded coconut, salt, and baking soda.
4. In a separate bowl, stir together the coconut oil, maple syrup, and honey.
5. Add the wet ingredients to the dry ingredients, and mix well.
6. Transfer ⅔ of the batter to the prepared pan, and press it down with the back of a spatula. Spread the blackberry and chia mixture on top, following with the rest of the batter.
7. Bake for 20-25 minutes, or until the top turns golden brown. Allow the pan to cool for 15 minutes before cutting it into bars.

Nutritional Facts (62 g per single serving)
Calories 247
Fats 17 g
Carbs 23 g
Protein 3 g
Sodium 102 mg

Caramel Hemp and Chia Seed Popcorn

Servings: 4

Ingredients
8 cups popped unsalted popcorn
3 tablespoons maple syrup
2 tablespoons coconut oil, melted
3 tablespoons brown sugar
3 tablespoons hemp seeds
3 tablespoons chia seeds
¼ teaspoon ground nutmeg
¼ teaspoon salt

Preparation
1. Preheat the oven to 275°F. Line a baking sheet with parchment paper.
2. Place the popcorn in a large bowl. Coat it with maple syrup and coconut oil.
3. Scatter the sugar, hemp seeds, chia seeds, nutmeg, and salt over the popcorn. Toss to mix all the ingredients together. Transfer the popcorn mixture to the prepared baking sheet.
4. Bake for 20 minutes. Remove it from oven and allow it to cool before enjoying the crunchy popcorn.

Nutritional Facts (59 g per single serving)
Calories 289
Fats 18 g
Carbs 30 g
Protein 4 g
Sodium 150 mg

Lemon Chia Scones

Servings: 6

Ingredients
2 cups oat flour
1 tablespoon coconut flour
½ teaspoon baking powder
½ teaspoon baking soda
¼ teaspoon salt
¼ cup chia seeds
¼ cup coconut oil, solid (refrigerate if necessary)
¼ cup honey
1 egg
½ teaspoon vanilla extract
1 tablespoon lemon juice
1 tablespoon lemon zest

Glaze:
2 tablespoons nut butter
1 tablespoon honey
1 tablespoon coconut oil, melted
1 teaspoon lemon juice

Preparation
1. Preheat the oven to 350ºF. Line a baking sheet with parchment paper.
2. In a food processor, combine the oat flour, coconut flour, baking powder, baking soda, salt, and chia seeds. Give it a few pulses to combine everything together.
3. Crumble the solid coconut oil into the food processor. Give it another few pulses before adding the honey, egg, vanilla extract, lemon juice, and zest. Whizz the ingredients together until a dough forms. Let it sit for 5 minutes to allow the coconut flour to absorb the moisture.

4. Transfer the dough to the prepared baking sheet. Shape it into a round disc about 1 inch thick. Cut the dough into 6 equal triangles.
5. Bake for 15 minutes, until the dough is lightly browned. Remove the tray from the oven. Run a knife through the dough to carefully separate the scones, leaving at least 1 inch of space between each piece. Return the pan to the oven to crisp up for another 3-5 minutes.
6. Allow the scones to cool completely on a wire rack.
7. Meanwhile, prepare the glaze. In a small bowl, whisk all the ingredients together until it becomes smooth. Drizzle over the cooled scones

Nutritional Facts (114 g per single serving)
Calories 452
Fats 22 g
Carbs 55 g
Protein 13 g
Sodium 112 mg

Cauliflower Chia Patties

Servings: 30

Ingredients
½ head cauliflower, florets only
½ cup mozzarella
½ cup diced onions
¼ cup chopped parsley
1 large egg
Egg white from 1 large egg
3 tablespoons ground almonds
2 tablespoons cornmeal
2 tablespoons chia seeds
Salt and pepper, to taste

Preparation
1. Preheat the oven to 400°F. Line two baking sheets with parchment paper.
2. Bring a pot of water to a boil, then add the cauliflower florets and cook until they are tender, about 5 minutes. Drain the pot and run the cauliflower under cold water to stop the cooking process.
3. In a food processor, combine the cauliflower, mozzarella, onions, and parsley. Whizz all the ingredients until they are finely chopped. Transfer the cauliflower mixture to a clean bowl.
4. Add the egg, egg white, ground almonds, cornmeal, chia seeds, salt, and pepper to the cauliflower mixture, and combine until it reaches a batter-like consistency.
5. Scoop a tablespoon of the batter onto the prepared baking sheet, and lightly flatten it to form a disc. Repeat the same process until all the mixture is used up.
6. Bake for 16-20 minutes, flipping the rounds halfway through. Remove them from oven when they are golden brown.

Nutritional Facts (20 g per single serving)
Calories 24
Fats 1 g
Carbs 2 g
Protein 1 g
Sodium 19 mg

Crunchy Chickpeas with Chia Seeds

Servings: 2

Ingredients
1 (15 ounce) can chickpeas, drained and rinsed
1 tablespoon coconut oil, melted
1 tablespoon chia seeds
¼ teaspoon sea salt
½ teaspoon pepper

Preparation
1. Preheat the oven to 425°F. Line a baking sheet with parchment paper.
2. In a large bowl, toss together all the ingredients. Transfer them to the prepared baking sheet.
3. Roast them in the oven for about 20 minutes, or until they are golden brown. Remove them from the oven and allow them to cool down completely.
4. Enjoy them immediately, or store them in a tightly sealed container in the refrigerator for up to 2 weeks.

Nutritional Facts (241 g per single serving)
Calories 301
Fats 15 g
Carbs 34 g
Protein 13 g
Sodium 915 mg

Apricot and Chia Nut Balls

Servings: 17

Ingredients
¾ cup dried apricots
¼ cup cashews
¼ cup pistachios, shelled
¼ cup unsweetened, shredded coconut
½ tablespoon vanilla extract
1 tablespoon water
2 tablespoons cocoa powder
1 tablespoon honey
1 tablespoon cacao nibs
1 ½ tablespoons chocolate chips
1 tablespoon chia seeds

Preparation
1. In a food processor, blend the apricots, nuts, and shredded coconut until it becomes a paste. Transfer it to a bowl.
2. Mix in the vanilla extract, water, cocoa powder, honey, cacao nibs, chocolate chips, and chia seeds.
3. Scoop a tablespoon of the paste out using a spoon and roll it into a ball. Repeat the process until all the paste is used up.
4. Refrigerate for at least an hour for the bites to firm up before enjoying. Store them in the fridge for up to a week.

Nutritional Facts (25 g per single serving)
Calories 125
Fats 8 g
Carbs 13 g
Protein 2 g
Sodium 3 mg

Ginger Nut Chia Balls

Servings: 16

Ingredients
1 cup ground almonds
3 tablespoons fresh ginger
½ teaspoon ground cinnamon
1 cup dates, pitted
5 tablespoons nut butter
½ cup chia seeds

Preparation
1. In a food processor, blend together the ground almonds, ginger, cinnamon, dates, and nut butter, until the mixture reaches a paste-like consistency.
2. Divide the paste into 16 portions and roll them into balls. Scatter the chia seeds over the balls.
3. Refrigerate the balls overnight to let them firm up.

Nutritional Facts (31 g per single serving)
Calories 135
Fats 8 g
Carbs 15 g
Protein 4 g
Sodium 2 mg

Dessert Recipes

Cherry Chia Seed Pudding

Servings: 4

Ingredients
½ cup chia seeds
2 ½ cups unsweetened almond milk
½ cup sweet cherries, pitted and halved
½ teaspoon ground cardamom
1 teaspoon maple syrup
1 teaspoon vanilla extract

Preparation
1. Place the chia seeds in a medium-sized bowl.
2. In a blender, combine the milk, cherries, cardamom, maple syrup, and vanilla extract, and blend until the mixture is completely smooth. Pour the liquid over the chia seeds and give it a good stir using a fork.
3. Place the chia mixture into the refrigerator, and allow it to sit and thicken for at least 3 hours, or overnight.
4. Prior to serving, give the chia seed pudding a good stir to break up any clumps, and if necessary, thin the mixture down with more almond milk.

Nutritional Facts (218 g per single serving)
Calories 193
Fats 11 g
Carbs 20 g
Protein 6 g
Sodium 122 mg

Avocado and Chia Chocolate Mousse

Servings: 4

Ingredients

2 ripe avocados, peeled and pitted
⅓ cup honey
⅓ cup cocoa powder
3 tablespoons extra virgin coconut oil
1 teaspoon vanilla extract
½ teaspoon ground chia seeds
Optional topping: Cocoa nibs, whipped cream, chopped nuts

Preparation

1. In a food processor, blend all the ingredients until smooth, light, and fluffy. Scrape down the sides of the blender if necessary.
2. Transfer the mousse to 4 cups or ramekins. Refrigerate for at least 30 minutes to allow the chia to thicken.
3. Best serve chilled. Sprinkle it with your favorite toppings or nuts.

Nutritional Facts (146 g per single serving)

Calories 355
Fats 26 g
Carbs 36 g
Protein 4 g
Sodium 118 mg

Gluten-Free Chia Peach Cobbler

Servings: 9

Ingredients

3 cups peaches, pitted, peeled, and chopped
3 tablespoons chia seeds
⅔ cup warm water
2 cups almond flour
¼ cup coconut flour
½ teaspoon baking soda
¼ teaspoon sea salt
¾ cup honey
½ cup butter, softened
½ teaspoon vanilla extract

Preparation

1. Preheat the oven to 350°F. Lightly grease an 8x8 pan with butter.
2. Spread the chopped peaches in the bottom of the pan.
3. In a small bowl, stir together the chia seeds and warm water. Set them aside for 5 minutes to let them thicken up.
4. In a large bowl, whisk the almond and coconut flour with the baking soda and salt.
5. Pour the honey, butter, vanilla extract and chia gel into the dry ingredients, and mix thoroughly. Transfer the batter to the pan and spread it out to cover the peaches.
6. Bake for 30-45 minutes, or until the cobbler is golden brown. Leave it to rest for 10 minutes before serving it warm.

Nutritional Facts (135 g per single serving)
Calories 335
Fats 22 g
Carbs 35 g
Protein 6 g
Sodium 74 mg

Chocolate Chia Cookies

Servings: 10

Ingredients
1 cup almonds
1 cup hazelnuts
1 cup quinoa flour
⅓ cup maple syrup
5 Medjool dates, pitted
¼ cup water
3 tablespoons raw cacao powder
3 tablespoons chia seeds
2 tablespoons coconut oil

Preparation
1. Preheat the oven to 350°F. Line a 9x13 cookie sheet with parchment paper.
2. In a food processor, grind the nuts until they reach the consistency of fine flour. Add the rest of the ingredients and blend until they come together to form a dough.
3. Portion the batter using a tablespoon. Roll the batter into a ball and arrange it on the prepared cookie sheet, making sure to leave at least 1 inch of space in between each cookie. Using the back of the spoon, gently flatten the balls.
4. Bake for 20 minutes, or until the cookies firm up. Allow to cookies to sit on the sheet for 5 minutes before transferring them to a wire rack to cool down completely.

Nutritional Facts (83 g per single serving)
Calories 345
Fats 21 g
Carbs 35 g
Protein 9 g
Sodium 4 mg

Mocha Chia Seed Brownies

Servings: 16

Ingredients
¾ cup ground chia seed
¾ cup maple syrup
½ teaspoon baking soda
¼ teaspoon salt
½ cup butter
3 ounces unsweetened baking chocolate
¼ cup strongly brewed coffee
4 large eggs
2 ounces 70% dark chocolate chunks

Preparation
1. Preheat the oven to 350°F. Line a 9x9 pan with parchment paper and lightly grease the parchment with butter.
2. In a large bowl, whisk together the ground chia seed, maple syrup, baking soda, and salt.
3. Place the butter and baking chocolate in a microwave-safe bowl. Melt the chocolate on high for 1 minute. Take it out of the microwave and give it a good stir, until it becomes smooth and glossy. If there are still chocolate chunks, stick it back into the microwave for a 30 second interval, and stir again. Allow the chocolate mixture to cool down slightly.
4. Incorporate the coffee into the melted chocolate. Whisk in the eggs, and then add the chia mixture. Stir until all the ingredients are thoroughly mixed. Fold in the chocolate chunks, and transfer the batter to the pan.
5. Bake for 15 minutes. Remove the pan from the oven and let it cool completely. Cut the brownies into 16 squares, and serve.

Nutritional Facts (59 g per single serving)
Calories 219
Fats 15 g
Carbs 18 g
Protein 4 g
Sodium 61 mg

Raspberry and Coconut Chia Pudding Popsicles

Servings: 4

Ingredients
½ cup coconut milk
½ cup unsweetened almond milk
¾ cup raspberries
2 tablespoons chia seeds
1 tablespoon sweetened shredded coconut
4 teaspoons maple syrup

Preparation
1. In a large bowl, stir together all the ingredients. Cover the bowl with plastic wrap and refrigerate the mixture for 4 hours to allow the chia seeds to plump up.
2. Transfer the mixture to ice pop molds and freeze overnight.

Nutritional Facts (101 g per single serving)
Calories 142
Fats 10 g
Carbs 13 g
Protein 3 g
Sodium 34 mg

Orange Chia Seed Jelly

Yields 4 ½ cups

Ingredients
4 cups fresh orange juice, or any 100% fruit juice of your choice
1 ½ tablespoons gelatin
1 ½ tablespoons chia seeds

Preparation
1. Mix the chia seeds with 2 cups of the fruit juice. Set it aside to allow the chia seeds to thicken.
2. Meanwhile, heat the rest of the fruit juice in a medium saucepan over low heat until the liquid warms and begins to steam. Transfer it to a mixing bowl.
3. Stir in the gelatin until all the granules have dissolved.
4. Combine the chia mixture with the gelatin mixture and stir until the chia seed is evenly distributed throughout.
5. Place the bowl in the refrigerator to chill for at least an hour before serving.
6. Store any extra in canning jars with tightly fitting lids, for up to 10 days.

Nutritional Facts (177 g per single serving)
Calories 122
Fats 2 g
Carbs 25 g
Protein 2 g
Sodium 35 mg

Pumpkin Chia Seed Blondies

Servings: 9

Ingredients
2 tablespoons chia seeds
½ teaspoon baking soda
1 teaspoon baking powder
1 ¼ teaspoons ground cinnamon
¼ teaspoon ground ginger
¼ teaspoon nutmeg
⅛ teaspoon ground cloves
¼ cup coconut sugar
1 medium ripe plantain, peeled
1 cup pumpkin purée
2 tablespoons coconut oil, melted + more for greasing

Preparation
1. Preheat the oven to 350°F. Grease an 8x8 pan with coconut oil.
2. Whisk the chia seeds, baking soda, baking powder, spices, and sugar together.
3. Place the plantain in a clean bowl. Mash it with the back of a fork and add it to the dry ingredients.
4. Add the pumpkin purée and coconut oil, and combine until smooth. Transfer the batter into the prepared pan.
5. Bake for 20 minutes, or until a toothpick inserted in the center comes out clean.

Nutritional Facts (60 g per single serving)
Calories 101
Fats 4 g
Carbs 16 g
Protein 1 g
Sodium 3 mg

Fruit Salad with Chia Yogurt Dressing

Servings: 4

Ingredients

1 grapefruit, peeled
1 pear, cored
1 orange, peeled
1 avocado, peeled and pitted
1 mango, peeled and pitted
10 strawberries, hulled
Juice of ½ a lemon
¼ cup low fat Greek yogurt
2 tablespoons vanilla extract
¼ cup chia seeds

Preparation

1. Prepare the fruits by cutting them into bite-sized pieces. Transfer them to a large bowl.
2. Toss the fruits with the lemon juice, yogurt, vanilla extract, and chia seeds, making sure to coat each piece of fruit.
3. Serve immediately or chill in the refrigerator for 30 minutes.

Nutritional Facts (310 g per single serving)
Calories 280
Fats 14 g
Carbs 40 g
Protein 7 g
Sodium 13 mg

Quinoa and Chia Brittle

Servings: 10

Ingredients
½ cup uncooked quinoa
¾ cup pecans, chopped
¼ cup rolled oats
2 tablespoons chia seeds
2 tablespoons coconut sugar
2 tablespoons coconut oil
½ cup maple syrup

Preparation
1. Preheat the oven to 325°F. Line a baking sheet with parchment paper.
2. In a large bowl, mix together the quinoa, pecans, rolled oats, chia seeds, and sugar.
3. In a small saucepan, heat the coconut oil and maple syrup over medium-low heat for 2-3 minutes, or until the oil has emulsified.
4. Drizzle the wet ingredients over the dry ingredients, and stir to combine.
5. Spread the mixture in an even layer on the prepared baking sheet.
6. Bake for 15 minutes, or until the brittle is amber brown and fragrant. Turn the tray while baking to prevent the sugar from burning.
7. Let it cool completely before crushing it into bite-sized pieces.

Nutritional Facts (46 g per single serving)
Calories 198
Fats 11 g
Carbs 24 g
Protein 3 g
Sodium 3 mg

Recipe Index

Breakfast Recipes _____ 5
   Apple Chia Oatmeal _____ 5
   Overnight Chia and Berry Parfait _____ 6
   Tropical Chia Seed Breakfast Bowl _____ 7
   Gluten-Free Blueberry Chia Pancakes _____ 8
   Basic Almond Chia Granola _____ 9
   Chia and Egg Breakfast Cups _____ 10
   Banana Walnut Chia Bread _____ 11
   Whole Wheat Chia Waffles _____ 13
   Eggless French Toast _____ 14
   Peanut Butter and Chocolate Chia Muffins _____ 15
   Chia Seed Omelette with Mushrooms and Asparagus _____ 17
   Creamy Blueberry, Chia, and Coconut Smoothie _____ 18
   Peach and Chia Seeds Smoothie _____ 19
   Raspberry Chia Seed Jam _____ 20
   Spiced Plum and Pear Chia Seed Jam _____ 21
Savory Recipes _____ 23
   Chia Crusted Baked Tilapia _____ 23
   Salmon and Haddock Chia Fish Cakes _____ 24
   Chicken Chia Nuggets _____ 25
   Chia Breaded Chicken Breast _____ 26
   Red Curry Chicken with Chia _____ 27
   Beef and Broccoli Stir Fry _____ 29
   Meatloaf with Chia Seeds _____ 30
   Pulled Pork with Barbecue Chia Seed Sauce _____ 31
   Berry and Spinach Salad with Chia Seed Vinaigrette _____ 32
   Lamb Shank with Chia Seeds _____ 33
   Mushroom Pizza with Chia Seed Crust _____ 35
   Lentils and Chia Seed Stew _____ 37
   Baked Beef and Chia Meatballs _____ 38
   Superfood Burger Patties _____ 39

Salads, Sides, Snacks and Appetizers — 41
Cauliflower Chia Soup — 41
Sugar Snap Peas and Green Bean Chia Salad — 42
Grilled Fruits and Vegetable with Zesty Chia Dressing — 43
Blackberry Oat Bars — 45
Caramel Hemp and Chia Seed Popcorn — 46
Lemon Chia Scones — 47
Cauliflower Chia Patties — 49
Crunchy Chickpeas with Chia Seeds — 50
Apricot and Chia Nut Balls — 51
Ginger Nut Chia Balls — 52
Dessert Recipes — 53
Cherry Chia Seed Pudding — 53
Avocado and Chia Chocolate Mousse — 54
Gluten-Free Chia Peach Cobbler — 55
Chocolate Chia Cookies — 56
Mocha Chia Seed Brownies — 57
Raspberry and Coconut Chia Pudding Popsicles — 58
Orange Chia Seed Jelly — 59
Pumpkin Chia Seed Blondies — 60
Fruit Salad with Chia Yogurt Dressing — 61
Quinoa and Chia Brittle — 62

More Books by Sarah Spencer

Appendix - Cooking Conversion Charts

1. Measuring Equivalent Chart

Type	Imperial	Imperial	Metric
Weight	1 dry ounce		28g
	1 pound	16 dry ounces	0.45 kg
Volume	1 teaspoon		5 ml
	1 dessert spoon	2 teaspoons	10 ml
	1 tablespoon	3 teaspoons	15 ml
	1 Australian tablespoon	4 teaspoons	20 ml
	1 fluid ounce	2 tablespoons	30 ml
	1 cup	16 tablespoons	240 ml
	1 cup	8 fluid ounces	240 ml
	1 pint	2 cups	470 ml
	1 quart	2 pints	0.95 l
	1 gallon	4 quarts	3.8 l
Length	1 inch		2.54 cm

* Numbers are rounded to the closest equivalent

2. Oven Temperature Equivalent Chart

Fahrenheit (°F)	Celsius (°C)	Gas Mark
220	100	
225	110	1/4
250	120	1/2
275	140	1
300	150	2
325	160	3
350	180	4
375	190	5
400	200	6
425	220	7
450	230	8
475	250	9
500	260	

* Celsius (°C) = T (°F)-32] * 5/9

** Fahrenheit (°F) = T (°C) * 9/5 + 32

*** Numbers are rounded to the closest equivalent

Printed in Poland
by Amazon Fulfillment
Poland Sp. z o.o., Wrocław

50081807R00043